LLANDUDNO'S STORY

Michael Senior

Printed and published by
Gwasg Carreg Gwalch, 12 Iard yr Orsaf,
Llanrwst, Wales LL26 0EH
☎ *(01492) 642031   Fax: 01492 641502*

ISBN: 0-86381-391-7

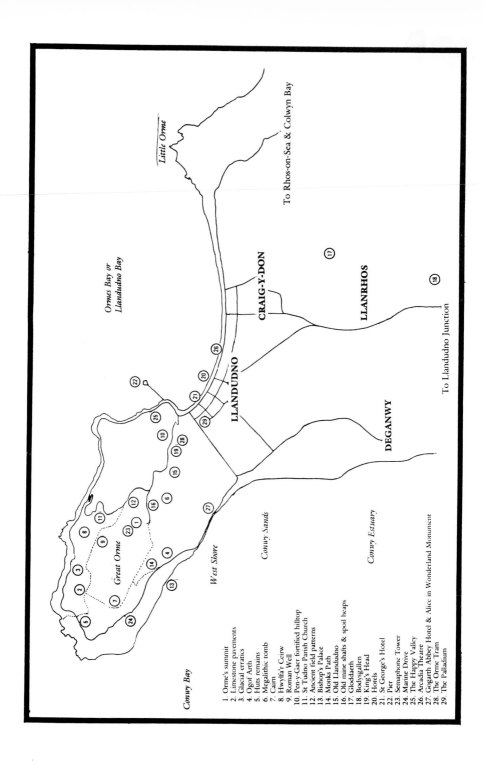

Little Orme

To Rhos-on-Sea & Colwyn Bay

Ormes Bay or
Llandudno Bay

CRAIG-Y-DON

LLANRHOS

LLANDUDNO

DEGANWY

To Llandudno Junction

Conwy Bay

Ormes Bay or
Llandudno Bay

Great Orme

West Shore

Conwy Sands

Conwy Estuary

1. Orme's summit
2. Limestone pavements
3. Glacial erratics
4. Ogof Arth
5. Huts remains
6. Megalithic tomb
7. Cairn
8. Hwylfa'r Ceirw
9. Roman Well
10. Pen-y-Gaer fortified hilltop
11. St Tudno Parish Church
12. Ancient field patterns
13. Bishop's Palace
14. Monks Path
15. Old Llandudno
16. Old mine shafts & spoil heaps
17. Gloddaeth
18. Bodysgallen
19. King's Head
20. Hotels
21. St George's Hotel
22. Pier
23. Semaphonic Tower
24. Marine Drive
25. The Happy Valley
26. Arcadia Theatre
27. Gogarth Abbey Hotel & Alice in Wonderland Monument
28. The Orme Tram
29. The Palladium

Preface to the Revised Edition

In the ten years since I first published this booklet there have been changes in Llandudno, most of them good.

The biggest change is undoubtedly the opening of The North Wales Theatre. This has, by itself, turned Llandudno into the cultural centre of North Wales, giving us a venue for orchestras and companies of world status, as well as a North Wales home for the much-acclaimed Welsh National Opera, and also enabled the institution of the town's 'October Festival'. With a new leisure and performance centre planned, this trend towards quality entertainment seems assured to continue.

It must be said, though, that this is only one side of Llandudno's coin. The relentless surge of out-of-town superstores has at the same time threatened its previous role of North Wales's shopping centre. Possibly as a result of this a stretch of Mostyn Street has succumbed to the invasion of the standardised fascias of multiple chain stores, and at present as I write (though we must hope this destruction can be reversed) almost a whole block of that once-fine piece of townscape would be disgrace, garish with crude colours and window posters, to any High Street in the country, let alone to the traditions of this one.

In the meantime the hand of Civic vandalism (by omission and commission) has added its destructive touch. There are few of the fine Victorian lamp-standards left now, because they were allowed to decline to irreparable decay. A failure of positive action somehow also allowed the historic Pier Pavilion to deteriorate and eventually be destroyed. We have not been well served, we might well think, in the recent past, by our Council officers. They are to blame as well (and this time by direct commission of Civic vandalism) for the obtrusive and ineffective 'sea defences' which have all-but wrecked the West Shore, the same result being only narrowly averted on the lovely sweep of the North Shore itself.

Let me not end this Preface to the update of *Llandudno's Story* on a sour note. Overall the town has retained, increased perhaps, its pride in itself, and mine in it. With enough fine features and well-kept elegance this stylish Victorian lady still makes me more than glad to remind people, whenever I can, that this is the town where I was born.

Michael Senior,
Glan Conwy, July 1996

CARBONIFEROUS LIMESTONE

BOUT three hundred million years ago this part of the world was tropical, and largely covered by warm shallow seas. Evaporation of these caused the precipitation of calcium carbonate, giving a succession of deposits which now form layers of a stone known as carboniferous limestone. The fine headlands flanking Llandudno, the Great and the Little Orme, are composed of these. You can clearly see the horizontal stata out of which they were built up.

This period ended about two hundred and eighty million years ago, and since that time these great outcrops have again and again witnessed scenes of massive change. Much of this change still shows here today. The bending and buckling of the earth's surface has tilted and folded their layers. The enormous rise and fall in sea level (itself caused both by the forming or melting of ice elsewhere, and by the sinking and rising of the land) is evidenced by the presence of fossils of sea creatures near the Orme's summit itself. (1) The small pockets in the limestone pavements are caused by a chemical corrosion due to the reaction between salt which settles there and the lime in the rock, and their extent on the Orme makes it seem possible that these slabs were once a beach. And everywhere across them a network of lines is scored, made by stones dragged over them under the pressure of thousands of feet of ice. (2)

The ice flowed over the Orme from different directions at different periods, and the lines on the rock record this. The great glaciers which formed the cwms and valleys of the Carnedd mountains joined in the lower Conwy valley and flowed here into the sea. Towards the end of the Ice Ages (the last of which took place between 60,000 and 10,000 B.C.) large amounts of ice broke loose from the Scottish icefields and flowed south down the Irish Sea. This, known as Irish Sea ice, carried on its surface boulders which had fallen there, and as it eventually melted it left these standing where we find them, looking oddly out of place, today. This explains the quantity of perched boulders, or 'glacial erratics', which are a feature of the top of the north corner of the Great Orme. (3)

Limestone is porous, so that there are no streams on the Orme, but instead a number of springs break out further down, from deep under the layers where the limestone rests on older rock. The 'wells' of Ffynnon Gogarth above the Marine Drive on the promontory's southern side, and nearby Ffynnon Llygaid (the 'eye well', from the supposed healing properties of its heavy copper content) are examples. Limestone is also subject to erosion at its faults, its

Limestone Pavements

'Glacial Erratics'

Fossils near the
Great Orme's summit

CARBONIFEROUS LIMESTONE

fissures easily becoming ravines, and the pounding of the sea and gnawing of salt gives rise to deep caves. There are many such on the Orme, but the most easily visible is perhaps the 'bear's cave', near the southern lodge of the Marine Drive, the Welsh name of which, Ogof Arth, is thought to have given the 'Gogarth' district its name. (4)

Llandudno owes much to this geological heritage. The limestone gives the broad platform of the Orme its natural terraces and its close springy turf. Limestone reflects the ultra-violet in sunlight, and thus adds a special intensity and clarity to the light, and above the Orme on a fine day a remarkable depth of blue to a clear sky. It is said also to give rise to negative air ions, which could explain the delicious freshness of Llandudno's air.

It was also the limestone which made the headland of the Orme an ideal site for early habitations.

'Ogof Arth' The Bear's Cave

7

6

THE FIRST INHABITANTS

HEN much of the lower land was covered in forest and dense scrub, human settlements tended to occur either above a certain height or on exposed seaward headlands, where the salt in the air discouraged the growth of trees.

The porous limestone of the Orme was a further discouragement to vegetation, and the sheltered platforms of the layers it provided must have presented a rare combination of ideal living conditions.

We can see the remains of such a settlement now alongside the Marine Drive at its north-west corner, where some large circles in the turf and among the bracken were the stone bases of huts. (5) This is a form of dwelling which was in use both during the Bronze and Iron Ages, and the probability is that this area was inhabited over a long period. In even earlier times, before the use of metal and the organisation to which that gave rise, the people lived in caves and rock shelters, and we know from recent finds that this area had been inhabitated probably from the Upper Paleolithic period (about 10,000 B.C.), through the Mesolithic to the New Stone Age. So-called 'Beaker' pottery (of between 2,300 and 1,700 B.C.) and Bronze-Age artefacts have been discovered in recent years on the slopes around Llandudno, and a famous find of human and animal bones dating to the New Stone Age was made in 1879, in a cave near to Ty Gwyn Road, at the south-east side of the Orme.

We would be able to infer the presence here of ancient man from the other evidence these people left. Until the construction of the Marine Drive destroyed some of them there were several megalithic tombs on the Orme, dating from possibly about 2,500 B.C. One of these still remains to show us the work of this early culture. Known as 'Llety'r Filiast', 'the lair of the greyhound bitch', it is to be found near the terraced houses below the Orme tram's half-way station, at the end of a short road called after it, Cromlech Road. (6) Although it was probably originally covered with a soil mound, its present bareness shows the structure of uprights and flat capstone characteristic of these tombs. The capstone was originally larger, as may be seen from the broken portions lying about the tomb.

That was the style of burial at that time, in strong stone structures used over a long period, presumably as communal graves for people of some standing. Perhaps a little later (or it could be by a different contemporary culture) burials were marked by the erection of a huge cairn, or mound of stones. An example of such a cairn, probably a burial of the Bronze Age, lies near the extreme western edge of the Orme's plateau. (7)

Although there is no sign on the Orme of the habitations of these people of

THE FIRST INHABITANTS

the Bronze Age, there is increasing evidence of their activities there, in the mining of copper ore. The Great Orme Exploration Society has now uncovered evidence for some 1,300 years of prehistoric mining, going back to 1,800 B.C., during which time it is estimated that between 10,000 and 50,000 tonnes of ore were extracted from the Orme. This makes this site one of the largest and oldest pre-historic mine-workings in the world and of unique value to our knowledge of pre-history. By itself it has thrust the start of the Bronze Age back nearly a thousand years.

One of the continuing puzzles about the Orme mines is the complete lack of evidence of smelting. Since to smelt that amount of ore would require the use of nearly a million tonnes of timber, the evidence for it should be easy to spot. The smelting must therefore have taken place elsewhere, and an incidental outcome of this conclusion is that the same team have started investigating the Bronze Age coastline, which they have shown to be considerably further out than that of today. Exploratory trips in 1996 cast new light on the legendary city of Llys Helig, which is said to lie out in Conwy Bay, including the first-ever investigation of it at low tide from the air. While no certain evidence has emerged yet that this reef of rocks in man-made, there are promising, or tantalising, signs of straight lines and right-angles.

A mysterious avenue of stones, returning to the Orme, known as Hwylfa'r Ceirw, 'the path of the deer', presumably from these early times, lies on the northern side of the plateau. (8) Apparently a ceremonial or ritual route, it runs straight towards the sea and ends at the edge of the escarpment.

Not far from this unusual feature, set into the wall which surrounds the top of the Orme, is a spring known as the Roman Well, said to have been used by the Romans to wash copper ore. (9) The original well lies the other side of the wall. It is known that much of the Roman activity in Britain was motivated by the desire for minerals, and there is evidence that they had discovered the rich copper seams of the Great Orme. Roman pottery and coins of the reign of Aurelian (270-5 A.D.) have been found in connection with the mines here.

At about the time of the Roman occupation of Britain, and for a period before and after, the inhabitants of this area lived in circular fortified enclosures set defensively on the tops of hills. An example of one of these occurs in a particularly prominent position, overlooking the modern town and its bay, at the south-east side, between the Happy Valley and the Wyddfyd Road. (10) Known as Pen-y-Dinas, it is now largely overgrown with thorn trees and its encircling rampart can hardly be seen. This single bank of earth and small stones is most easily visible on the south-east side, while on the north-east, just to the south-east of a break caused by the modern pathway, it may be seen to consist of limestone slabs. Inside the hillfort a number of round huts have been identified.

Bronze Age Cairn

The Roman Well

'Hwylfa'r Ceirw'

Pen-y-Dinas, Iron Age Fort

11

EARLY CHRISTIANS

NY visitor to Wales will be struck by the frequency with which Welsh placenames begin with the word 'Llan'. This is because so many settlements are based on ancient Christian foundations. 'Llan' is usually translated as 'church' or 'parish', but means an area associated with a church or religious settlement, originally a sanctified enclosure; and the second part of the place-name is the name of the founding 'saint', one of the pioneering Christians who set up small monastic groups in outlying parts of Britain's western lands, in the so-called 'dark' period between the Roman withdrawal and the Saxon invasions. In Llandudno's case the missionary 'saint' was Tudno, the 't' in his name having become mutated to a 'd' in accordance with a rule of grammar.

We do not know very much about Tudno. Later tradition gives him as one of the sons of a henchman of the king of Cantref Gwaelod, the area off the coast of Aberdovey said to have been inundated in the sixth century. Whatever his origins, it is likely that he brought Christianity to this area at about that time, and that in doing so he built a church and monastic compound on the spot now occupied by the Parish Church of St Tudno. (11) This forms a site of strong romantic atmosphere now, within sound of the sea, and no doubt Tudno chose it at least partly for its defensive outlook since sea-borne raiders were a severe problem in the centuries after the Roman withdrawal.

Tudno's church would have been made of wattle, and of course has not survived. Wooden churches were widely replaced by stone ones during the 12th century, and it is probably to this period that the oldest parts of St Tudno's belong. There is medieval stonework in the north wall of the nave, near to the porch, and probably the small window east of the porch belongs to the early building. The bulk of what is there now however dates from about 1500 or a little before, and some of the other windows are modern. The church was extensively repaired in 1855, after being damaged by storm.

Tudno's little monastic community would have to be self-sufficient, and no doubt a factor in the choosing of the site was the presence of sheltered and even land to farm. All around this area we can still see the marks of ancient field-patterns, the ridges left by strip cultivation and ploughing. (12) These persistent records left on the earth's surface were probably the product of centuries of use, and it is not usually possible to distinguish confidently between the pre-historic and the medieval.

If a religious community survived here throughout the period from Tudno's foundation to the building of the present church, one of the problems which

The Bishop's Palace

The Monk's Path

EARLY CHRISTIANS

they would have had to face would be the sporadic attacks of Vikings. These marauding voyagers were a fearful presence all round the British coast during the 9th, 10th and 11th centuries, and particularly in the Irish Sea, since what is now Dublin was for a long period a Viking city. Indeed the name 'Orme' itself is almost certainly of Viking origin, since it is an old Scandinavian word related to our word 'worm', and means a dragon or sea-monster, a reference to the appearance which such headlands as this (and Worm's Head on the Gower) take on when viewed from the sea.

In any case the religious presence here seems to have remained strong, and a fragment of ruin on the west shore of the Orme marks the site of a once-grand palace of medieval bishops. (13) It was probably first built in the 13th century, when the area was given to the Diocese of Bangor by Edward I, after his conquest of 1282, perhaps as a reward to Bishop Anian for christening his son, the future Edward II, who was born at Caernarfon. The bishop may well have built himself a fine seaside residence in his new territory, unfortunately choosing its site in such a way that most of it has since fallen into the sea. Signs of fire indicate that it was perhaps destroyed in the rebellion of Owain Glyndŵr in the early fourteen-hundreds, and it then became a ruin, being described by the historian Leland in 1536 as 'almost clene downe'. A path known as the Monk's Path rises across the slope above the old palace, being said to be the route from there to the church. (14) The fact that it stays green even in a severe drought is said traditionally to be due to its having been trodden by the feet of holy men.

OLD LLANDUDNO

I N The Great Orme Mines Museum there is a large copper ingot believed to have been smelted on the Great Orme by the Romans. Certainly, as has been said, there is evidence of their mining here, and this rich seam of copper could indeed account for their continued presence at Canovium, now Caerhun, on the Conwy river. Pre-historic finds including implements apparently designed for digging indicate that the Romans were exploiting an industry already established, and it very probably continued here ever since then.

It was the 18th century which saw the great expansion of mining everywhere, partly caused by a general economic and trading expansion, and faciliated by the introduction in the early years of that century of the use of gunpowder.

The land on the Orme where the ore was most accessible belonged to the Bishop of Bangor, and Mostyn land also began to be worked nearby, the work expanding dramatically during the 1830's. Flooding of both workings led to their combining to bore a half-mile drainage tunnel from the West Shore, which then became a tracked extraction route.

It was during the late 18th and early 19th centuries, due to the increasing activity at the mines, that Llandudno really came into existence. This forerunner of the town we know was perched high on the slopes of the Orme, in the form of terraces of small cottages, often tucked into sheltering valleys. (15) These degenerated into slums after the mines had closed, but are now much sought-after and almost everywhere renovated and modernised.

Profits from the 'Old Mine' declined during the 1840's, but a further venture, the Tŷ Gwyn Mine, had by then come into existence, this time in the Happy Valley area, above the Grand Hotel. This flourished for a time, but its success was curtailed by flooding, in this case with sea water. Pumps installed near where the Empire Hotel now is ultimately failed to keep this at bay, and the Tŷ Gwyn Mine closed during the 1840's being flooded in 1844, briefly opened again in 1846 and was then quite overwhelmed by the breaking-in of the sea.

That was virtually the end of mining at Llandudno, though some work continued at the Old Mine and its neighbour, the 'New Mine', until the end of the 1850's. The success, though brief, had been dramatic. It is estimated that ore worth the equivalent of £1½ million in current terms had been extracted before the decline in the mid 1840's.

Today we can see the results of all this mainly in the terrace cottages of the old town, and above them the shafts and spoil heaps still visible around the

Terraced Cottages on the Orme

Gloddaeth Hall

18

tram's half-way station, together with many indentations left by the pits of trial borings and the installations of machinery. (16)

To understand how Llandudno developed from that point, and achieved its ultimate character, one must bear in mind that it has from the start been in the control of one family, the Mostyns, who still hold the ground leases of most of its property. The fortunes of the town and the Mostyns have been consistently intertwined, to the benefit of both.

The great families of Wales date the origins of their status to the period of the reign of Henry VI, in the first half of the 15th century, when central control collapsed so far as to put the effective power of government into the hands of the gentry. At that time the ancestors of the Mostyns were landowners in the area of Llangollen, and in the 1450's acquired by marriage the estate of Gloddaeth, in what was then Caernarfonshire, where the present house (now St David's School) was built as a Mostyn home in the 16th century. (17)

Later, in the 18th century, Sir Roger, the fifth baronet, acquired by marriage the estate of Bodysgallen (where the partly 17th century house is now a hotel) in the same area, formerly a property of the other prominent North Wales family, the Wynns. (18) It was thus that considerable property in the Llandudno area became vested in Sir Roger Mostyn's grandson, who was created first baron Mostyn in 1831.

By the time he died, in 1854, Llandudno had undergone a radical change from mining village to fashionable resort.

VICTORIAN
WATERING PLACE

 LANDUDNO owes its origins and success as a major seaside resort to a fortunate convergence of a whole set of varied factors.

The habit itself of 'bathing', in the sense of immersing yourself in water for the beneficial physical effects, had become fashionable, as part of a general concern with health and well-being, during the 17th and 18th centuries — though the habit was much favoured by the Romans, who tapped mineral springs throughout Europe, and had probably never died out. Those who could afford the time and expense formed the custom of spending some weeks of the year at 'spa' resorts (so called after the town of Spa in Belgium) such as Bath and Tunbridge Wells. This in itself gave rise to the practice of going on holiday, a period of rest and relaxation away from one's routine cares which would in any case be salutary, the good effects of the trip presumably being hard to distinguish from those of the waters which provided its purpose.

Since some of the best of these beneficial waters, such as those at the spa of Droitwich, were very strong in brine, or salt solution, it must have seemed a reasonable next step to start immersing oneself, for health reasons, in the sea itself.

Proximity to a prosperous population gave the south coast of Britain its usual advantage, and royal visits to Brighton and Weymouth made those towns into fashionable resorts by the end of the 18th century. Bournemouth followed in 1810. Blackpool, however, though a bathing spot since the 1780's, did not develop into a residential resort until the coming of the railway in 1846. In 1801 it had a population of only 473, so that presumably the bathers resorting to it lived within a day's journey.

Two factors changed this pattern. The industrialisation of the north took its most striking form in the vast expansion of Manchester, in combination with its port of Liverpool, at the start of the 19th century. This in turn gave rise to a new, and numerous, prosperous class. At the same time technological improvments gave to this new class greatly improved mobility. Telford built highroads from the Midlands and north-west into North Wales in the 1820's and 30's. But most crucially mobility, previously the privilege of the few, was extended to the population as a whole by the coming of the railway in the 1840's. The main line to Holyhead was in operation by 1848, and the Llandudno branch line followed ten years later.

Opp.: The King's Head   21

Two old prints showing the growth of the resort

VICTORIAN WATERING PLACE

In those ten years the seaside resort of Llandudno had come into existence. Until the 1830's Llandudno was a cluster of terraces of miners' cottages in a cleft of the Orme, served by the King's Head public house (19), overlooking a long stretch of sandbanks and shingle where only an occasional fisherman's hut broke the bleakness. Any interest there might have been in the place centred on the activities of the mining company, then still flourishing. The sandy waste was common land, and of apparently little value, so that there can have been no resistance to the enclosure order which awarded it to the Mostyn family, as local landowners, by an Act of Parliament of 1843.

The very next year the idea of a resort was born. The series of events leading to its birth has the air of a folk tale, and it may be that it had been incubating in the minds of the Mostyns and their advisers for some time. In 1844 the mining town was visited by an architect from Liverpool, Owen Williams, who is said to have suggested over dinner in the King's Head that the site would be ideal for a watering-place. The secretary of the Tŷ Gwyn mining company, John

St George's Hotel

23

Llandudno today

Williams, also the Mostyns' agent, was present at the meal, and he quickly put this idea to Lord Mostyn. In due course he became the secretary of the Improvement Commission which governed the development of the town. This was strictly controlled by an Act of Parliament of 1854, devised by the Hon. E.M.L. Mostyn, who was also the area's M.P.

In the meantime a town plan had been commissioned from Messrs. Wehnert and Ashdown, and on the basis of this 176 plots of land were offered for auction, at the end of August 1849.

The new town started at the front, and to begin with there was no more to it than a short thin line of hotels facing the bay. (20) The first of the seafront hotels to be completed was the St George's, which opened its doors in 1854. (21) Development of the rest of the town centre took place over the next thirty years, but its extension westwards and south to the West Shore and Craig-y-Don is a feature belonging to this century. It dates in its first phase from the 1850's, and in its essence as a town it belongs to the 1880's.

The subsequent development of the town followed the lines laid down from the start, with a firm grid-pattern of streets and ample spaciousness in layout. It is thanks to all the careful plans and to the strict control which has governed it from the start that Llandudno is as it is. To this day it remains as much as

VICTORIAN WATERING PLACE

anything an elegant and almost untouched example of Victorian confidence in the future.

22

OUR PRESENT HERITAGE

LTHOUGH Llandudno's nature thus became established as a leisure area, it might well not have been so. The intention in the 1850's was that it should become a working port. The first pier, built in 1858, was to have served shipping, and the coming of the railway was originally part of a plan to make Llandudno's bay into the main port for Ireland.

There was considerable competition for this role during those decades. Although the railway to Holyhead was built by 1850 it was still hoped in 1853 that it might be diverted to Llandudno, and the port built there. A set-back occurred when a storm damaged the pier, and the branch-line which was built in 1858 came to serve the emerging resort, just as the new pier constructed in 1875 was for explicitly pleasure purposes. (22)

This second pier, with further embellishments, was, and still is, a notable success. In the 1880's the largest swimming pool in the country was built below the Pier Pavilion ('admission, including Pier, 6d.') at the shoreward end of the pier. By 1891 the permanent population of the town was 7,333, a figure which the 1895 North Wales edition of the 'Thorough Guide Series' claims would need to be 'multiplied by at least three if it is to represent the condition of things at the height of the season', giving an impressive summer population of some 22,000. 'The popularity of the place is easily accounted for,' continues the guide, in words still very relevant, 'and is the product of three main factors — the situation of the town, its first-class provision for the health and comfort of visitors, and its convenience as a base for excursions.'

In the meantime however the maritime role made inevitable by its jutting coastal position continued in the background. The wreck of the brig Hornby, on New Year's Day 1824, which left only one survivor, is still remembered in the name of the Hornby Cave, in the cliffs of the north-west corner of the Orme. The lighthouse, recently closed but for many years the first sight of home for trans-Atlantic liners heading for Liverpool was opened in 1862. A more remarkable result of this key position at the approach to the great port of Liverpool was the Orme's-head semaphore, the tower of which is still a part of the building at the Orme's summit. (23)

This was built by the Trustees of Liverpool Docks in 1826 as part of a chain of signals stretching from Holyhead, where the first siting of an arriving ship was made, via points in Anglesey and along the northern coast, through Hilbre Island and Bidston Hill to the Old Tower Building in Liverpool. A message usually took four to five minutes to pass from Holyhead to Liverpool, though at a demonstration run in 1830 it made the journey in a remarkable 23

The Happy Valley

The Gogarth Abbey Hotel

28

seconds. The semaphore was replaced by electric telegraph in the late 1840's, and the building eventually became a hotel, the 'Telegraph Inn', which also served as the clubhouse of a small golf-course on the Orme's plateau until requisitioned as a radar station during World War Two.

In the 1870's the Orme, originally circuited by a rough path, was made accessible to all by the construction of the Marine Drive. (24) The Mostyns then gave to the town its major public park, the Happy Valley, which was laid out in the late 1880's. (25) The second pier planned for the centre of the bay never emerged, but the shore pavilion which was to be its first phase was built in 1894, and became until its demolition the Arcadia Theatre. (26) Behind it the ambitious Edwardian addition, the Grand Theatre, belonging to the early years of this century, had in recent decades fallen on hard times and is now a successful night club.

The West Shore meanwhile remained largely neglected, in spite of its magnificent view, probably because of the great expanse of mud left at the ebb of the huge tides of the estuary. However in the 1860's it attracted the attention of Thomas Liddell, Dean of Christ Church, Oxford, who built there a holiday home now forming part of the Gogarth Abbey Hotel. (27) The fact would be of little interest, had not his daughter Alice formed the model for Lewis Carroll's much-loved 'Alice in Wonderland', published in 1865. Though Alice herself spent childhood holidays with her family here, it must be said that the movements of all concerned are fairly well documented, and there is no evidence that Lewis Carroll ever came with them.

Yet another unusual feature of the town, and an enhancement of its character as an all-round pleasure resort, came into being at the beginning of this century. The attractive funicular known as the Orme tram (28) was opened in the summer of 1902, making it nearly forty years younger than its better-known counterpart in San Fransisco. With the exception of one accident in 1932 (due to the emergency brakes having been disconnected) the line has functioned successfully in its original form ever since, and is operated now by the County Borough Council.

The town continued to expand in the early part of this century, the West Shore and Craig-y-Don residential areas being added after the First World War, making it as much a place for people to move to live in as to visit on holiday. To this period, the 20's and 30's, belong the great places of entertainment, such as the Odeon cinema (now demolished and replaced with flats) and the magnificent Palladium built in 1920. (29) Before the last war Llandudno was both smart and popular. Ward Lock's guidebook of 1934-5, when a room with breakfast at the Marine Hotel on the promenade cost 6/-,

The Orme Tram

The Palladium

OUR PRESENT HERITAGE

remarked that although Llandudno contained over 2,000 hotels and boarding-houses, 'those are wise who book their accommodation well in advance.'

The coming of cheap air fares has changed all that. It may be that the bucket-and-spade days are over, the sandcastles and the donkey-rides on the beach. To some extent of course foreign travel is a two-way process, and Llandudno offers the pleasure of its beauty and its historic charm to those who, perhaps lacking it at home, may appreciate it more than we do. Undoubtedly its best hope in the long run lies in its sheer quality, the unmatched setting, the sweep of its fine facade and the spaciousness of its streets. As such elegance and style become more rare there is already in progress a trend towards the greater appreciation of such things, and with this return to old values Llandudno seems poised to take part in yet another boom. Unless those who control it prove unusually shortsighted, it stands to benefit once again from its first planners' taste for the decorative and the well-made.

ACKNOWLEDGEMENTS
The author wishes to record his debt to Mr Tom Stone, local historian
and amateur archeologist, for information on recent archeological
discoveries in the Llandudno area.

PICTURE ACKNOWLEDGEMENTS
Aerial view of the Orme: University of Cambridge; No. 17: St David's College
All the others by the author.

Also by Michael Senior

A widely published historian with a series of well written volumes
about different areas of North Wales.

THE CONWY VALLEY - ITS LONG HISTORY
48pp, 0-86381-035-7   £1.50

ANGLESEY - THE ISLAND'S HISTORY
64pp, 0-86381-389-5   £2.75

DISPUTED BORDER
The North Wales Marches   48pp, 0-86381-125-6   £1.75

CONWY - THE TOWN'S STORY
32pp, 0-86381-345-3   £1.95

CAERNARFON - THE TOWN'S STORY
32pp, 0-86381-346-1   £1.95

THE CROSSING OF THE CONWY
From prehistoric times to the new tunnel.
112pp, 0-86381-191-4   £3.75

NORTH WALES IN THE MAKING
A guide to the area's early history. Hard-back.
128pp, 0-86381-322-4   £9.75